ESSENTIAL  DK MANAGERS

MANA
YOUR TIME

TIM HINDLE

DORLING KINDERSLEY
London • New York • Sydney • Moscow

A DORLING KINDERSLEY BOOK

Project Editor Sasha Heseltine
Project Art Editor Ellen Woodward
Designers Elaine C. Monaghan,
Austin Barlow
Assistant Editor Felicity Crowe
Assistant Designer Laura Watson

DTP Designer Jason Little
Production Controller Alison Jones

Series Editor Jane Simmonds
Series Art Editor Jayne Jones

Managing Editor Stephanie Jackson
Managing Art Editor Nigel Duffield

First published in Great Britain in 1998
by Dorling Kindersley Limited,
80 Strand, London WC2R ORL

8 10 9 7

Copyright © 1998
Dorling Kindersley Limited, London
Text copyright © 1998 Tim Hindle

Visit us on the World Wide Web at
http://www.dk.com

A CIP catalogue record for this book is available
from the British Library

ISBN 0 7513 0530 8

Reproduced by Colourscan, Singapore
Printed in China by Wing King Tong

CONTENTS

MAKING INSTANT CHANGES

MANAGING THE TIME OF OTHERS

INTRODUCTION

Everybody has to manage their time to some extent whether it be at home or at work – or both. The sequence in which you perform tasks on an everyday basis has a profound effect on how much you get out of life. Most people have the capacity to manage their time better, and doing so makes the working day more productive and leisure time more fulfilling. Manage Your Time shows how you can improve your own use of time. It is full of practical advice to help you, and 101 concise tips are scattered throughout the book giving further vital information. It begins by examining how you currently manage your time, and looks at the areas that need improvement. It then tells you how to do this in fast, easy stages from how to deal with paperwork to how to communicate in a time-efficient way. The last chapter shows you how to use your new knowledge to help others manage their time more efficiently.

UNDERSTANDING TIME

Time is our most valuable resource. By analyzing time usage on a regular basis, it is possible to understand the most efficient ways to use time, both in and out of the workplace.

ANALYZING TIME

People's attitudes towards time are complex and variable. If you want to use your time efficiently to accomplish all that you need to do at work and at home, you need to be aware of the current habits and attitudes that shape your use of time.

1 Set aside time each day to review and prioritize demands on your time.

CULTURAL DIFFERENCES

Perceptions of time and its usage vary worldwide. Differences are often reflected in the average number of hours worked per day or week, the importance of punctuality, or time spent on leisure activities. Be prepared to adapt to others' practices and timetables when working abroad.

CHANGING ATTITUDES

Our attitudes to time are constantly changing. Many of these changes are due to the advent of new technology, which affects our work, travel, and communication. The Internet, e-mail, and modems have made the exchange of information almost instantaneous. Travel, especially over long distances, has become faster and more affordable. The increase in options available has made it possible for us to do more in a day, but has also increased the pressure on our time. This makes it all the more important to use time in the most efficient and productive way.

USING TIME WISELY

Everybody is increasingly aware of the cost of time. Individuals and departments are held accountable for their use of time: goals are clearly defined and financial penalties are incurred for missed deadlines. Company culture can have an important influence on how employees use their time. In too many organizations, working long hours is equated with working hard; if you leave on time, others may think you are not pulling your weight. In fact, long hours often decrease efficiency and productivity. Ways of using time become habitual, so make an inital investment of time to rethink and improve these habits. The rewards will be the ability to control your workload, and more time to focus on the most important aspects of your job.

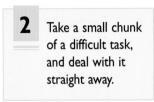

2 Take a small chunk of a difficult task, and deal with it straight away.

▼ MANAGING QUERIES

A manager who is constantly interrupted has little time for substantial tasks, while staff who must always consult their manager for decisions and information are held up. Use planning and delegation to minimize time-wasting at every level.

Subordinates waste time waiting for manager's attention

Colleague needs clarification and authorization from manager

Manager neglects own tasks while dealing with queries from other staff

ANALYZING USE OF TIME

Few of us will readily admit that large parts of our working day are wasted. The only way for you to make better use of your time is to analyze how you use it now, and then to consider ways in which you can reallocate it in a more effective way.

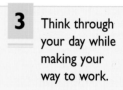

3 Think through your day while making your way to work.

ASSESSING YOUR DAY

There are always competing demands on your time. It is very easy to spend too much time on routine things, such as reading mail, at the expense of high-priority, productive tasks. How do you divide up your day at the moment? Do you prioritize your work so that you tackle important and urgent projects first? Or do you concentrate on completing enjoyable tasks first? Are you distracted by phone calls, or do you have a system for dealing with them? Do you waste a lot of time?

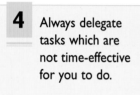

4 Always delegate tasks which are not time-effective for you to do.

COSTING YOUR TIME

It is a sobering exercise to calculate exactly how much your time costs and then realize how much of it is not being spent effectively. Use the calculation on the right to work out how much your time at work costs per hour and per minute, and then use these figures to analyze the relative cost of a few activities typical of your day, such as arranging a meeting yourself rather than asking your assistant to undertake that task. Always consider whether you should delegate tasks to others: it is generally more cost-effective to give routine tasks to more junior staff rather than doing them yourself, since your cost to the company will be higher.

▼ **ESTIMATING VALUE**
To find out the cost of each minute of your time, multiply your annual salary by 1.5 – to include overheads – and divide the total by the number of working hours in a year (workings hours per week times working weeks per year). Divide this total by 60.

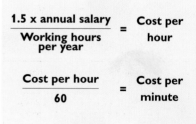

$$\frac{1.5 \times \text{annual salary}}{\text{Working hours per year}} = \text{Cost per hour}$$

$$\frac{\text{Cost per hour}}{60} = \text{Cost per minute}$$

KEEPING A TIME LOG

Maintaining a daily log of how much time you spend on particular activities is fundamental to managing your time more effectively. You may be surprised at how much time you spend chatting, and how little time you spend working and planning. Your time log provides you with a starting point from which you can assess areas to improve. How long you should keep a time log for is dependent on the nature of your work. If you work on a monthly cycle, keep the log for a couple of months. If your work cycle is weekly, a two- or three-week log should suffice.

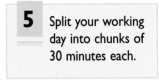

5 Split your working day into chunks of 30 minutes each.

▼ **TIMING TASKS**
Compile a simple time log by dividing your day into 30-minute chunks and recording exactly how you spend your time. This will help you determine how much time you spend on useful and unnecessary tasks.

Time	Monday
8.30	*Train to work – looked at papers and stared out of window.*
9.00	*Went through mail. Chatted with Steph over coffee.*
9.30	*Read some e-mails.*
10.00	*Regular Monday progress meeting – started 10 minutes late.*
10.30	*Continuation of meeting. Phoned Mary to confirm lunch.*
11.00	*Started writing up list of things to do.*
11.30	*Read more e-mails and responded to a few.*
12.00	*Phoned suppliers about late deliveries.*
12.30	*Travelled to Mary's office for working lunch. Bus late. Wasted 15 minutes.*
1.00	*Had working lunch with Mary to discuss her promotion prospects. Got distracted.*

Time	Monday
1.30	*Lunch with Mary continued. Did not talk about work.*
2.00	*Travelled back to office.*
2.30	*Organized desk. Made cup of coffee. Read more e-mails and responded to Alec's.*
3.00	*Called Jim about Thursday's meeting. Started to write two letters. Robert rang.*
3.30	*Phoned Anna about international sales. Talked about her family for 15 minutes.*
4.00	*Discussed today's progress meeting with Bill and Emma.*
4.30	*Started to write up progress reports, including data from today's meetings.*
5.00	*Checked e-mails again. Refiled some untidy documents on screen.*
5.30	*Booked restaurant for tomorrow's lunch with Philippa.*
6.00	*Took work home on train. Fell asleep.*

REVIEWING A TIME LOG

To analyze your time log, allocate all of the 30-minute time chunks that you have recorded into categories according to the nature of each task, and calculate the amount of time spent on each type of task, such as meetings, reading and replying to mail, helping colleagues, or making phone calls. Now calculate the percentage of your time spent on each task. This will give you a better picture of your working day and will enable you to assess how you can allocate your time more effectively.

6 Review your time log to assess your work efficiency.

7 Allow for some thinking time in your schedule.

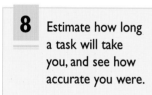

8 Estimate how long a task will take you, and see how accurate you were.

BREAKING DOWN TASKS

Look at the categories into which you have allocated your tasks, and divide them into groups: routine tasks (for example, writing a regular report), ongoing projects (for example, organizing a meeting), and tasks that would further develop your job (for example, making new contacts). Work out the percentage of time spent on each group.

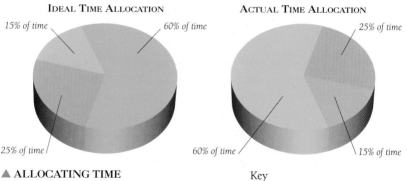

IDEAL TIME ALLOCATION

15% of time   60% of time

25% of time

ACTUAL TIME ALLOCATION

25% of time

60% of time   15% of time

▲ ALLOCATING TIME

To be most effective in your job, you should spend about 60 per cent of your time on Group 3 tasks, 25 per cent on Group 2 tasks, and only 15 per cent on Group 1 projects. In fact, most people allocate their time in exactly the opposite proportions: 60 per cent on Group 1, 25 per cent on Group 2, and 15 per cent on Group 3.

Key

■ *Group 1: Routine tasks*

■ *Group 2: Ongoing projects*

■ *Group 3: Planning and development*

LOOKING FOR PATTERNS

Now that you have established how your time is being allocated, ask yourself if the breakdown meets your expectations of your working day. Are you spending too much time on Group 1 tasks rather than concentrating on important Group 3 jobs? Look at the distribution of these tasks throughout your working day. Are there times when you are very busy and others when you are slack? If so, try to find ways to reorganize your working day so that you are able to work more consistently and efficiently, and achieve more.

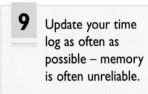

9 Update your time log as often as possible – memory is often unreliable.

QUESTIONS TO ASK YOURSELF

Q Do I do work that should be done by somebody else?

Q Are there patterns that repeat themselves in my time log? Am I always involved in Group 1 tasks in the morning?

Q Do jobs frequently take longer than I expect them to?

Q Do I have enough time to be creative and innovative?

ESTIMATING EFFICIENCY

How close is your work pattern to the ideal 60:25:15 time distribution ratio shown on the facing page? If you find you are spending too much time on one group of tasks to the detriment of others, work out how you can reorganize your daily schedule so that your time is distributed more efficiently. For example, if you find you are spending time on tasks that could easily be done by a junior, delegate them. This way you can concentrate your energies on the areas in which you are not spending enough time.

REVIEWING YOUR USE OF TIME

SHORT TERM
Once you have analyzed your use of time, there are several time-saving strategies you can implement immediately:
- Make a list of things to do, and update it several times a day;
- Look on your time log at wasted time and think of ways to fill those time slots more constructively in the future.

LONG TERM
If you find you have long-term problems, try changing your work patterns more radically:
- Pinpoint all the work patterns you are unhappy with. In particular, look for any bad habits you have slipped into.
- Once you have identified these problem areas, set aside time to rethink and improve your approach.

ASSESSING YOUR ABILITY

The key to successful management is the possession of good time-management skills. Find out how well you manage your time by responding to the following statements, and mark the options that are closest to your experience. Be as honest as you can: if your answer is "never", mark Option 1; if your answer is "always", mark Option 4; and so on. Add your scores together, and refer to the Analysis to see how you scored. Use your answers to identify the areas that need most improvement.

OPTIONS
1 Never
2 Occasionally
3 Frequently
4 Always

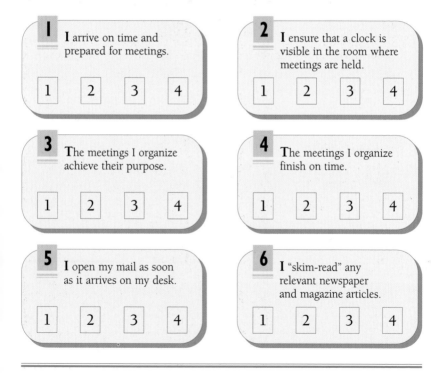

1 I arrive on time and prepared for meetings.

1 2 3 4

2 I ensure that a clock is visible in the room where meetings are held.

1 2 3 4

3 The meetings I organize achieve their purpose.

1 2 3 4

4 The meetings I organize finish on time.

1 2 3 4

5 I open my mail as soon as it arrives on my desk.

1 2 3 4

6 I "skim-read" any relevant newspaper and magazine articles.

1 2 3 4

7 I cross my name off the circulation list for magazines and journals I do not read.

| 1 | 2 | 3 | 4 |

8 I read my faxes on the day on which I receive them.

| 1 | 2 | 3 | 4 |

9 I am able to complete tasks without interruptions from colleagues.

| 1 | 2 | 3 | 4 |

10 I decide how many times I can be interrupted in a day.

| 1 | 2 | 3 | 4 |

11 I reserve certain hours for visits from colleagues.

| 1 | 2 | 3 | 4 |

12 I close my office door when I want to think strategically.

| 1 | 2 | 3 | 4 |

13 I tell telephone callers that I will return their calls, and do so.

| 1 | 2 | 3 | 4 |

14 I limit the duration of my telephone calls.

| 1 | 2 | 3 | 4 |

15 I allow a colleague or secretary to screen my telephone calls.

| 1 | 2 | 3 | 4 |

16 I decide how many telephone calls I can deal with personally in a day.

| 1 | 2 | 3 | 4 |

17 I "skim-read" internal memos as soon as I receive them.

1   2   3   4

18 I read internal memos thoroughly later.

1   2   3   4

19 I keep the contents of my in-tray to a manageable size.

1   2   3   4

20 I clear my desk of all paperwork.

1   2   3   4

21 I delegate tasks to colleagues that I could do myself.

1   2   3   4

22 I follow up on the work I have delegated.

1   2   3   4

23 I encourage subordinates to limit their reports to one side of paper.

1   2   3   4

24 I consider who needs to know the information I am circulating.

1   2   3   4

25 I achieve the right balance between thinking-time and action-time.

1   2   3   4

26 I make a list of things to do each day.

1   2   3   4

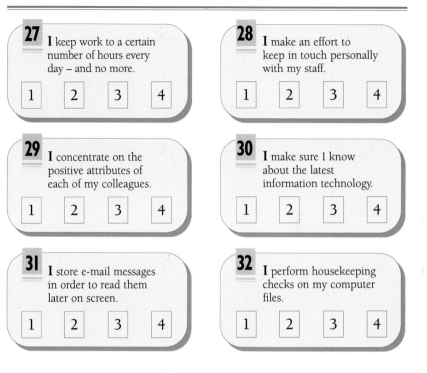

27 I keep work to a certain number of hours every day – and no more.

1   2   3   4

28 I make an effort to keep in touch personally with my staff.

1   2   3   4

29 I concentrate on the positive attributes of each of my colleagues.

1   2   3   4

30 I make sure I know about the latest information technology.

1   2   3   4

31 I store e-mail messages in order to read them later on screen.

1   2   3   4

32 I perform housekeeping checks on my computer files.

1   2   3   4

ANALYSIS

Now you have completed the self-assessment, add up your total score and check your performance by reading the corresponding evaluation. Whatever level of successful time management you have achieved, it is important to remember that there is always room for improvement. Identify your weakest areas, and refer to the sections in this book where you will find practical advice and tips to help you establish and hone those skills.

32–64: Learn to use your time efficiently, and reduce the time you spend working in unproductive and labour-intensive ways.
65–95: You have reasonable time-management skills, but they could improve.
96–128: You use your time very efficiently; keep looking for new ways to further streamline your work practices.

PLANNING FOR SUCCESS

You cannot decide what to deal with today unless you know where you want to be tomorrow. Any plan to improve your use of time depends on being clear about your goals.

ANALYZING YOUR GOALS

Long-term personal and professional goals are essential when it comes to setting overall targets. But in the short term a personal goal, such as starting a family, may take temporary precedence over long-term aims such as running a business.

10 Break down long-term plans into weekly and daily action plans.

BALANCING GOALS

Short-term professional goals

Long-term professional goals

Short-term personal goals

Long-term personal goals

SETTING GOALS

Write down all your goals and then divide them into short and long term, personal and professional. Consider whether your goals are realistic: while you cannot change your physical attributes, you can learn new skills at any time. Think about which skills you need to acquire to achieve the goals you have set. As the traditional idea of one job for life disappears, you may have to update certain skills in order to remain employable, and this means your professional goals can be richly varied. Finally, set a timetable – decide when you would like to achieve each of your goals.

PLANNING CAREER GOALS

To help you achieve your goals, it is important to make long- and short-term career plans that you can bear in mind as you plan your use of time from day to day. You may find it useful to write down your experience, skills, and qualifications. As well as work, you may have acquired valuable management experience from running the home or looking after siblings. Looking at these skills and experience, list all the careers to which they would be relevant.

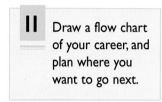

11 Draw a flow chart of your career, and plan where you want to go next.

CHARTING YOUR WORKING LIFE

Start first job or apprenticeship

Work in finance or accounts department → *Take evening classes*

Start a family ← **Join the company's biggest customer** *Meet students in other lines of work*

Take maternity or paternity leave

Work in sales and marketing → *Take a management course*

Broaden horizons ← **Gain work experience abroad** *Apply for promotion*

Cultivate useful contacts

Set up and run own business

WORKING OUT PRIORITIES

*Once you have listed your long- and
short-term professional goals, you need
to arrange them in priority order. Each goal
will involve the successful completion of a
number of tasks. Decide which tasks are the
most important and need urgent attention.*

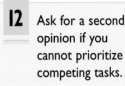

12 Ask for a second
opinion if you
cannot prioritize
competing tasks.

POINTS TO REMEMBER

- Your employer's priorities may
  not be the same as your own.
- Priorities change. They may
  need to be reassessed at the
  beginning of every day.
- The closer you are to achieving
  your goal, the more important it
  is to prioritize and concentrate
  on the tasks in hand.

13 Identify conflicts of
priority between
you and your boss.

ANALYZING YOUR WORK

Be as honest as possible about your current job.
How much of your time is spent doing the wrong
task at the wrong time, and missing the goals you
have set for that day? If you have 10 objectives to
achieve each day, ranging from the mundane and
routine to the urgent and complex, which of these
takes priority? Analyze your working day, and
decide which of your projects are routine, which
concern ongoing or mid- to long-term projects,
and which are extremely urgent and important,
or due for imminent completion. Whatever your
position within your workplace, the careful
planning and organization of your day will make
all the difference to your efficiency at work, and
how successful you are at achieving your goals.

ANALYZING TASKS

Make a list of all your current, upcoming, and
routine goals and tasks. Then divide them into
three categories – Type A, B, or C:
- Type A: tasks that are important and urgent;
- Type B: tasks that are either important or
  urgent, but not both;
- Type C: tasks that are neither important
  nor urgent, but routine.
If you are in any doubt about how to categorize
a specific task, consider it a C-task, or discard it.

14 Find out whether
your colleagues'
priorities conflict
with your own.

PRIORITIZING AND DELEGATING WORKLOAD

To work out your specific priorities, look again at your task list. Now make three separate lists – one each for A-, B-, and C-tasks. Starting with the A-tasks, work through the lists, deciding which tasks need input from others, which ones only you can do, and which can be delegated. Consider whether any tasks are unnecessary, and discard them. Involve people with the tasks that require outside input, and hand over jobs that can be delegated immediately. This will leave you with three shorter lists of A-, B-, and C-tasks that only you can do, enabling you to go to the next step: planning your day. By estimating how long it might take you to complete each of these tasks (noting down timings next to each item), you will be better placed to begin coordinating contributions from colleagues, fitting your tasks around organized meetings, and planning longer-term projects.

15 Classify all work engagements in your diary according to their importance.

16 If your schedule is full of A-tasks, then delegate or redefine them.

BALANCING DAILY TASKS

A-TASKS
You should try to complete a few of these urgent, difficult tasks each day.

ONE WORKING DAY

C-TASKS
These are non-urgent tasks that should be done when time allows.

B-TASKS
These account for the majority of your work and should take up most of your day.

PLANNING YOUR DAY

Any working day should include a mixture of A-, B-, and C-tasks. Plan a selection of tasks that you can realistically achieve in one day, while making sure that the working day does not stretch to 20 hours. Spread the three types of tasks throughout the day, rather than working in sequence through all the A-tasks followed by B-tasks, and so on. This way, you can intersperse blocks of intense concentration (devoted to A-tasks) with periods of less demanding B- and C-tasks.

PRIORITIZING A TASK

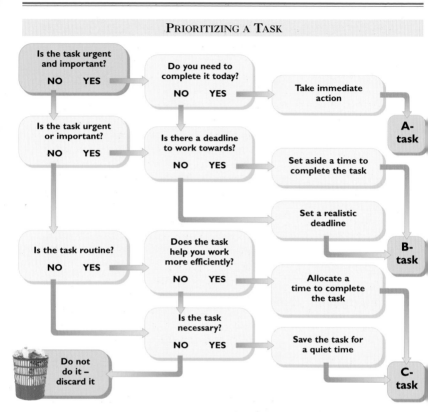

BALANCING DEMANDS

Priorities change all the time because we receive information all the time, whether from the Internet, the telephone, or a colleague popping their head around the door. New information may change a task's importance or urgency. It may push an urgent job off your critical list. Why prepare a report for a meeting scheduled for tomorrow when it has been postponed for three days? When you receive any new information, quickly reassess your list of priorities.

> **17** Alter priorities continually in line with changes or new information.

- Time spent on drawing up a plan is never a waste – it will save you time in the long run.

- Avoiding burn-out is achieved by pacing yourself for a working life, not just a working day.

- Time management is doing things more effectively, not just more quickly.

- Food is vital for concentration levels and health – regular refreshment breaks are important.

- Quiet times in the office, such as before everyone has arrived, can be used to great effect.

18 To keep discussions short, avoid open-ended questions.

BEING REALISTIC

There are few things more stressful than exaggerated expectations, so be realistic about what you can achieve in a given period of time. You will not benefit yourself or your colleagues by embarking upon a punishing and overambitious schedule that you cannot maintain. Learn to recognize the limits of your capabilities, and do not undertake a project that you know you cannot complete successfully. Likewise, try to be realistic in your expectations of others. Do not demand too much from your colleagues, or you will be frustrated by their inability to complete the jobs you have given them, and they will soon become exhausted and demoralized. Once you have established what is reasonably achieveable – whether for yourself or for others – stretch your expectations from time to time. People sometimes need to feel stretched and challenged when at work, and they want to enjoy the satisfaction of having achieved something that is a little bit beyond their expectations and experience.

BOOKING QUIET TIME

You need some time to yourself – time to collect your thoughts, assess priorities, and concentrate on difficult or high-priority tasks. This quiet time will not become available unless you schedule it into your day. Do not feel guilty about shutting yourself off from your colleagues. Explain that they can have your full attention once you have had a short period of time free from interruptions and distractions. This is particularly important if your workplace is noisy and chaotic. Try to be self-disciplined, and use this time constructively to tackle A- or B-tasks that need your undivided attention. Remember that even a short period of quiet time will help you work more efficiently.

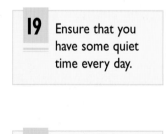

19 Ensure that you have some quiet time every day.

20 Do not be afraid to leave the phone off the hook.

ASSESSING WORK PATTERNS

Everybody has a natural daily rhythm to their energy patterns, rising to peaks of mental and physical performance, then experiencing troughs of low energy. Become familiar with your personal rhythm so that you can work with rather than against it.

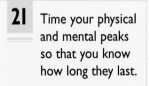

21 Time your physical and mental peaks so that you know how long they last.

TIMING TASKS

22 Keep some energy for home life and leisure activities after work.

It is important to allocate the most demanding tasks of the day to the times when you are at your physical and mental peaks. If you are the sort of person who gets up early and goes jogging at dawn, you should make sure that you complete most of your A-tasks early in the day. On the other hand, if you have difficulty in getting out of bed before 9 a.m., you should leave your A-tasks until the late morning or early afternoon.

TAKING BREAKS FROM CONCENTRATED WORK

It is important to schedule relaxation time into your day, because your concentration levels and productivity start to decline as you tire. Plan breaks in your personal work pattern to match the times when your energy levels are low. Remember, the average person can only concentrate intensively on work for one hour without a break.

RELAXING AT WORK ▶

When you take a break, let your mind and body rest. Relax at your desk by lowering your head and closing your eyes. Rest your hands on your thighs, and breathe deeply.

MAXIMIZING EFFICIENCY

Your performance levels will fluctuate according to when you feel energetic and alert, and when you feel tired. You need to understand the mental and physical cycles that your body follows each day in order to prioritize and plan your workload effectively. Note down the times at which you feel most tired or alert over a few days, and record the tasks you were performing at these times. If you were performing difficult tasks when you were tired, you were not working efficiently. In future, try to schedule easy C-tasks for these energy dips.

Because individual energy patterns can vary enormously, many companies now operate more flexible working hours. This allows employees greater control over their daily timetables and the opportunity to use time more efficiently by fitting work around their mental and physical cycles.

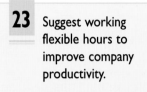

23 Suggest working flexible hours to improve company productivity.

▼ CHARTING PEAKS AND TROUGHS

Draw up a chart to show how your energy levels vary during a typical working day. Assign a number between 5 and -5 to your performance at every hour during the day (0 represents an average level of performance), and mark it on a graph as shown below. Join the marks to illustrate your energy cycle. Use this as a guide when scheduling your A-, B-, and C-tasks.

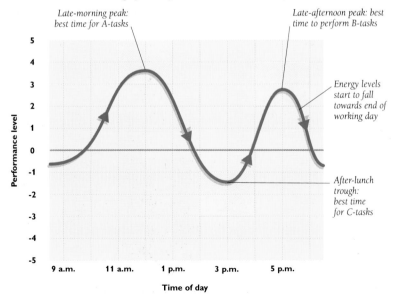

Late-morning peak: best time for A-tasks

Late-afternoon peak: best time to perform B-tasks

Energy levels start to fall towards end of working day

After-lunch trough: best time for C-tasks

Performance level — Time of day

USING TIME PLANNERS

K*eeping a reliable and precise record of forthcoming events, appointments, and obligations is crucial for efficient time management. There are many different types of planner available, so shop around to find the one that suits your needs best.*

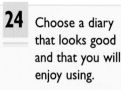

24 Choose a diary that looks good and that you will enjoy using.

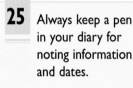

25 Always keep a pen in your diary for noting information and dates.

CHOOSING A SYSTEM

The traditional way to record future plans by hand is in a diary. Increasingly sophisticated personal planners and electronic organizers, with address books and accounting systems, are now available and are useful for keeping information to hand. The type you choose should depend on the work you need to organize. You may need a whole page for each day; or it might be more important to be able to see a week at a glance.

CHOOSING A TIME PLANNER

The type of time planner you choose will largely be a matter of personal choice. Each type, from the traditional diary to the high-tech electronic planner, has specific features to recommend it, so it is up to you to find which one suits you best.

▲ **STANDARD DIARY**
Record events and appointments in a diary as and when they are scheduled. It is a good idea to keep old diaries for future reference.

▲ **PERSONAL ORGANIZER**
Use a personal organizer as a diary, address book, weekly or monthly planner, and notebook.

▲ **ELECTRONIC PLANNER**
Store names, telephone numbers, addresses, appointments, and personal details in digital form.

PLANNING WITH A DIARY

Using a diary takes discipline. The first thing you need to do is to get used to taking the time to record appointments and scheduled events as and when they are made. Make a note of how long the preparatory steps prior to your meetings take, and remember to build in the time needed for preparation and travel before appointments, as well as for any follow-up or reporting afterwards.

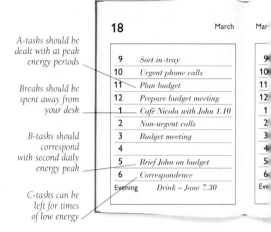

A-tasks should be dealt with at peak energy periods

Breaks should be spent away from your desk

B-tasks should correspond with second daily energy peak

C-tasks can be left for times of low energy

18	March	Mar
9	*Sort in-tray*	9
10	*Urgent phone calls*	10
11	*Plan budget*	11
12	*Prepare budget meeting*	12
1	*Café Nicola with John 1.10*	1
2	*Non-urgent calls*	2
3	*Budget meeting*	3
4		4
5	*Brief John on budget*	5
6	*Correspondence*	6
Evening	*Drink – Jane 7.30*	Eve

26 Use coloured pens to denote tasks of varying importance.

▲ USING A DIARY EFFECTIVELY

Take a look at the events scheduled for each day in your diary. Make sure that you have planned the right balance of tasks and taken into account a realistic assessment of your personal, mental, and physical energy patterns.

MAINTAINING A DIARY

If somebody other than yourself is responsible for the upkeep of your diary, let them know of any appointments as soon as you make them to ensure maximum efficiency and productivity. Make sure that you have access to the latest version of your diary, and that you check it at regular intervals to confirm your arrangements. Consider using an intranet system that can provide simultaneous access to a single electronic organizer from a number of different locations.

Each day, schedule important A-tasks around planned events, and make sure you complete them within a specified time. Remember to leave yourself enough slack time each day to deal with any unexpected situations that may arise.

ACCESSING INFORMATION

Take advantage of the speed with which electronic organizers can access data through their search facilities. By using key numbers and/or words, any information in the database can be called up almost immediately. Similarly, you can add a series of tabs to a personal organizer to help you open it quickly at particular days or letters of the alphabet.

MAKING A MASTER LIST

Having categorized all your jobs A, B, and C, according to urgency and importance, there may still be occasions when you feel confused about and overwhelmed by the number of projects that you face and the time you have in which to complete them. This is a good time to take a few minutes to make a master list, writing all your tasks on it, great and small, plus their deadlines. The very act of listing these important tasks is therapeutic and will take a weight off your mind. In addition, a list gives you a better overview of the whole situation than does a daily view of scheduled tasks. Certain solutions will suggest themselves; you may realize, for example, that the marketing plan for a new product that seemed to be way behind schedule can be postponed because the assembly line for the new product is itself running late.

▲ KEEPING UP TO DATE
Remember to add new items to your master list as soon as you receive them, and cross off any tasks once you have completed or delegated them.

POINTS TO REMEMBER

● Your master list should be consulted at the beginning of every day.

● Items should be crossed off your master list as and when they are done: it is very satisfying to see a list get shorter.

● At the end of each day, new items that have been added to a master list should be assessed and categorized as A-, B-, or C-tasks.

● Your master list can enable you to combine related tasks.

● When time is allocated for tasks on a master list, extra time should be left for unscheduled items.

● A master list of things to do at home should be kept, as well as a master list of work-related tasks.

USING LISTS EFFECTIVELY

Your master list should feature all your A-, B-, and C-tasks. Make the list living and ever-changing, crossing items off as you complete them, adding new tasks as they arise, and highlighting items as your priorities change. If you wish, group similar tasks together, for example, putting a star next to phone calls, a cross next to important letters to be written, and highlighting meetings to be arranged. This will help you to see at a glance what has to be done, and may encourage you to complete all similar tasks at the same time. You may save time at home if you also make a list of domestic tasks.

27 Set realistic deadlines. A deadline is meant to be helpful, not a major cause of stress.

28 Delegate enjoyable tasks as well as unpleasant ones.

29 Reward yourself when you meet your deadlines.

DOING UNPLEASANT JOBS

Tasks of different types suit different personalities. A job that you find particularly unpleasant, such as dealing with a difficult customer, for example, may be regarded as an enjoyable challenge by a colleague. There is nothing to be gained from performing unpleasant tasks for the sake of it, so if you can delegate appropriately, do so.

When it is unavoidable, try to do a difficult job when you are in a positive frame of mind. Do not put it off until the end of the day, when you may be tired, or wait until just before the deadline.

PLANNING LONG-TERM

Many tasks on your master list will not disappear when they are done. Tasks in the working year often recur in cycles – for example, you may want to aim a certain product at certain customers at the same time every year. To allocate regular time to recurring tasks, you need a long-term back-up to your short-term planner, such as a colour-coded wall chart. Use bright colours to map out regular events so that you can see how busy you are at a glance, and can plan ahead accordingly.

30 Plan your diary no more than one year ahead.

▼ PLANNING THE YEAR

List all regular events on a colour-coded wallchart, like the example below. Allocate the time needed for each in a different colour. This allows you to see if any events are overlapping and need to be rescheduled.

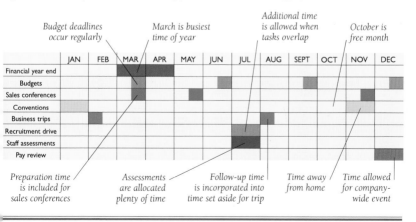

Budget deadlines occur regularly

March is busiest time of year

Additional time is allowed when tasks overlap

October is free month

	JAN	FEB	MAR	APR	MAY	JUN	JUL	AUG	SEPT	OCT	NOV	DEC
Financial year end												
Budgets												
Sales conferences												
Conventions												
Business trips												
Recruitment drive												
Staff assessments												
Pay review												

Preparation time is included for sales conferences

Assessments are allocated plenty of time

Follow-up time is incorporated into time set aside for trip

Time away from home

Time allowed for company-wide event

THINKING POSITIVELY

Time can sail past for some people and drag for others. Which of the two applies to you depends mostly on your attitude. Use the power of positive thinking to make your plans successful, and even the most distasteful of tasks will seem painless.

31 Make sure you do at least one thing every day that you enjoy.

ENJOYING LIFE

Different people have different ways of enjoying themselves, but if you do not make time to do the things you genuinely enjoy, your whole outlook can be adversely affected. Be aware of the tasks at work that give you particular pleasure, and make sure that they are well spread throughout your schedule. Plan regular leisure outings – to the cinema, music festivals, or motor racing. In addition, try to cultivate a positive outlook, even when not engaged in the tasks that give you particular pleasure.

32 Read a passage by your favourite author last thing at night.

LIVING WELL

The beginning and end of each working day are particularly important times. Start the day with a healthy, unhurried breakfast, and sit down while you are eating to allow you to relax and enjoy it more. Make sure that you leave yourself enough time to get to work without feeling rushed. At the end of the day, leave your workplace in a positive frame of mind. This will help to prevent the difficulties of the day from carrying over into your personal life. Make a conscious effort to relax and stop thinking about work at least two hours before you intend to go to bed.

◀ **EATING HEALTHILY**
Think carefully about what you are eating, and at what time of day. Ideally, your day should start with fresh fruit and cereals or bread, and finish with a light meal. Too much heavy food late at night can lead to insomnia, fatigue, and irritability.

DEALING WITH PROBLEMS

With a positive attitude to life, it is much easier (and quicker) to manage your time and solve problems at work. Start focusing on feeling good about yourself and your life, and you will be less likely to interpret the problems of others as your own. This will help you to be objective and constructive in coming up with methods of dealing with tight deadlines and budgets, and resolving conflict.

33 Concentrate on your colleagues' and clients' positive attributes.

CASE STUDY

Anthony, a sales executive, had been asked to attend a high-pressure meeting, which included staff from other departments among its participants.

A week before the meeting, Anthony realized that he had been convincing himself that it would go badly. He decided it was time to try to change his pattern of negative thinking into positive thinking.

First, he used various prioritizing techniques to ensure his material would be prepared well. Then, he set about positively visualizing the meeting and its outcome. He "saw" himself stand up, clear his throat, and give the report he had prepared. He then imagined himself successfully answering all of the questions that came from the other participants at the meeting. Finally, he visualized the approval on the faces of his colleagues, especially the ones that he usually felt intimidated by. On the day, the meeting went just as Anthony had imagined — and this boosted his confidence.

◀ **TAKING POSITIVE STEPS**
Anthony was creating a cycle in which his negative thinking was producing a negative outcome. His decision to change negative aspects into positive ones was conscious, but not easy to effect at first. Each success made it easier, and eventually the habit of positive thinking became automatic.

34 Use an organizer to list weaknesses, then plan how to combat them, one by one.

AVOIDING STRESS

By definition, busy people do not seem to have time to plan their future. It takes determination to find time in a busy schedule to think about how to use the next few hours productively. Psychologically, however, it is good practice to plan your activities because it enables you to be in command of your time, putting you back "in the driving seat" of situations that look as if they might go out of control. When you take the time to plan, you can consciously be positive – and this will help you avoid stress as well as achieve your goals.

MAKING INSTANT CHANGES

There are many practical things that you can do to improve your efficiency over the short and long term – from clearing a desk and keeping it tidy to streamlining computer systems.

CLEARING YOUR OFFICE

Efficient organization of your work space can make an enormous difference. Start with your desk, setting up a system to ensure that nothing is lost among growing piles of papers. Then tackle filing cabinets, bookshelves, and your general surroundings.

35 Keep your desk clear of everything but the current job in hand.

36 Beware of self-sticking notes. They are easily lost.

37 Clear up daily. Never leave a mess for the morning.

PROJECTING AN IMAGE

You can tell a great deal about the occupant of an office from the arrangement of items on the desk, the use of colour, and the general level of tidiness. Superiors, colleagues, and subordinates alike will form their first impressions of you from the state of your work space – so ensure that the impression you give is positive. If you regularly receive visitors at your desk, make sure that the image you are projecting is the one that you want them to see. You will never convince a well-organized outsider that an untidy work space reflects anything other than a disorganized mind.

Memos and junk mail cover computer

Reading material is stuffed into file and forgotten

Files are bulging and not kept up to date

Filing cabinets overflow with irrelevant information

Important contact name is stuck on side of computer

Papers obscure telephone

Waste paper covers floor

Waste bin needs emptying, as litter is overflowing

▲ WORKING IN CHAOS

The longer you delay tidying up your desk, the more difficult the job becomes, and the more likely it is that time will be wasted.

PROCESSING DOCUMENTS

Think of your desk as an assembly line. Raw materials (mostly in the form of paper) come in at one end to be processed by a machine (your mind) before they are sent off to the next stage. The just-in-time logistics that companies apply to manufacturing processes can also be applied to your desk. This means being aware of how urgent papers are and where they need to go. Glance at documents as soon as they come in: if they are urgent, take action or delegate at once. Place non-urgent papers that are waiting for something else before they can be processed into a pending tray, and put all other non-urgent papers into your in-tray to be processed next time you go through it.

THINGS TO DO

1. Keep work surfaces as clear as possible at all times.

2. Tidy desk drawers, and keep them ordered.

3. Keep pens, pencils, glue, and rulers together in a single, accessible container.

4. When not in use, place the computer keyboard out of the way to create more working space.

ORGANIZING PAPERWORK

Set up a system for keeping up to date with all the paperwork that appears on your desk. Deal with urgent items immediately. For non-urgent items, set aside some time each day to go through your in-tray. If you need to take any action, write it down on your master list of things to do. File away other items to read later (or keep them for reference), and throw away anything that you do not need or have already dealt with.

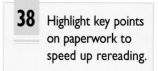

38 Highlight key points on paperwork to speed up rereading.

▼ PROCESSING PAPERS
Take time to process all incoming papers daily. Be disciplined, and follow this simple system to keep your desk clear.

Note action you need to take	→	Handle, file, or delegate	→	Throw away everything else

Only document being used is on screen

Files are up to date

In-tray contains only current paperwork

Out-tray is cleared frequently

Files used regularly are close to desk

Phone is easily accessible

Unnecessary items are thrown away

Files used most frequently are easiest to access

▲ KEEPING A CLEAR DESK
It is good use of time management to keep your desk clear. Using desk space efficiently will keep you better organized and able to find things quickly.

ORGANIZING WORK SPACE

The objects in your work space (desks, chairs, tables, filing cabinets, lamps) should be organized to suit you. Think about your work patterns and what you use your office for. If you have a lot of visitors, place your desk so that you can see the door and be aware of people approaching. If you regularly hold meetings in your office, arrange the furniture so that visitors can sit comfortably.

If possible, your work space should contain only those files to which you refer regularly. Keep these near your desk, preferably so that you do not need to stand up frequently to reach them. The files that you look at rarely should be put in a special storage space, or, if this is not available, in an out-of-the-way corner of the office.

39 Position a clock in your office so it is visible to you and to visitors.

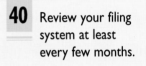

40 Review your filing system at least every few months.

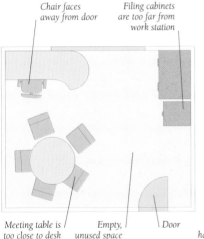

Chair faces away from door

Filing cabinets are too far from work station

Meeting table is too close to desk

Empty, unused space

Door

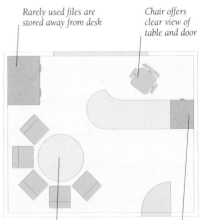

Rarely used files are stored away from desk

Chair offers clear view of table and door

Meeting table has ample space

Regularly used files are next to desk and give extra work space

▲ WASTING SPACE
The furniture in this office is arranged so that it is cramped in some areas and empty in others. The room must be crossed to reach the filing cabinets, while the meeting table is too close to the desk.

▲ CREATING SPACE
This arrangement makes a more efficient use of the space available. The table is well placed for meetings, and there is a good view of approaching visitors. Frequently used files are next to the desk.

FILING PAPERWORK

It is well worth taking time to set up an efficient filing system – think of the hours you can waste looking for something that has been stored at random. No one filing system is ideal. Choose one that is designed to suit the materials you need to store.

41 Set up a filing system that will grow with you and your business.

42 Go through your files regularly and discard documents that you no longer need.

ORGANIZING YOUR FILING

A filing system has to work in the same way as a computer's search function. Key words have to trigger off thought sequences in your brain that lead easily to the place where a paper is filed. Such sequences will be determined by the nature of your work. If you are an exporter with markets in 70 different countries, your basic classification may be along geographic lines, so you might have five big filing cabinets – one for each continent. If you are a sales manager for a small company producing stationery products, you may divide your customers into two filing cabinets – one for domestic customers, the other for overseas. Each customer will be allocated their own folder.

BREAKING SUBJECTS DOWN

If you have large categories in your files, it is a good idea to subdivide them to make them more manageable. For example, a development manager who is responsible for overseeing numerous projects could group files by individual project, and then subdivide each project into different sections, each with a separate file.

▼ SORTING FILES
Divide your files into categories on the basis of need, then store them accordingly. Keep those that you use all the time nearest to you and those that you refer to occasionally a little further away. The rest should be archived elsewhere or thrown away if they will not be used again.

Often need	Sometimes need	Archive

LABELLING CLEARLY

It is helpful to have a system that indicates immediately, by means of colour or typography, the level or classification of each file. For example, a sales manager could file documents relating to export customers in red files tagged with red labels and those relating to domestic customers in blue files with blue labels. Each label would be annotated with the name of a customer. Whatever system you adopt, it must be easily understood by you and any other users, so keep a printed list of the sections, subsections, and their contents for easy reference.

43 File papers with no obvious home in a folder labelled "Miscellaneous".

▼ COLOUR CODING
Using a system of colour coding allows you to locate files of a particular type at a glance. This reduces the time you spend searching for documents, thus increasing the efficiency of your working practices.

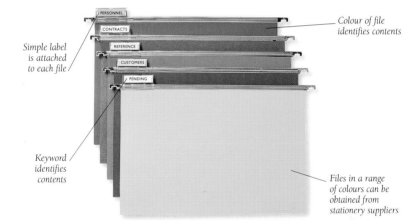

PERSONNEL
CONTRACTS
REFERENCE
CUSTOMERS
PENDING

Colour of file identifies contents

Simple label is attached to each file

Keyword identifies contents

Files in a range of colours can be obtained from stationery suppliers

FILING REGULARLY

Set aside a regular time for filing – either at the end of every day or at the end of each week. Do not always delegate the task of filing to someone else – it is useful for everyone to update their knowledge of the filing system. Decisions about what to keep and what to throw away are critical, so take an active part in deciding which documents are no longer required and should be discarded, and which are to be kept for future use.

44 File only essential documents that will be referred in the future.

AVOIDING INTERRUPTIONS

Sometimes interruptions are welcome, but everyone needs to work undisturbed at certain times. Make your working day as productive as possible by discouraging interruptions by colleagues, and reorganizing your office so that you are less visible.

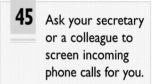

45 Ask your secretary or a colleague to screen incoming phone calls for you.

LISTING INTERRUPTORS

To reduce the number of unnecessary interruptions you receive, first draw up the following lists:
● People who may interrupt you at any time, such as your boss or important customers;
● People who may interrupt you when you are not particularly busy, such as colleagues;
● People who may not interrupt you at all.
Keep these lists in mind, and give copies to your support staff and relevant colleagues. Ask them to follow these lists as much as possible.

46 Pick up the phone to indicate the end of a meeting.

Visitor stands to one side of chair and must work hard to gain attention

DISCOURAGING ▶
INTERRUPTIONS
Use negative body language to fend off unwanted intrusions. Turn your head, but not your whole body, towards the visitor. Use signals such as glancing at your watch.

Head turns towards visitor

Arm and shoulder form a barrier, discouraging long discussion

Holding pen signals an unwillingness to be interrupted

RETHINKING WORK SPACE

You are especially vulnerable to interruptions if it is easy for passers-by to catch your eye. Position your desk so that you can see who is approaching the door. Keep your office door closed when you do not want to be interrupted. Even if you work in an open-plan office, you can minimize interruptions by making changes to the layout of your work space – repositioning your desk behind filing cabinets, for example, or placing your computer monitor directly in front of you. Once you make yourself less visible to staff and colleagues, they are less likely to disturb you unnecessarily.

47 Do not sit down if you are followed into your office.

48 Place your chair out of view if your door is open.

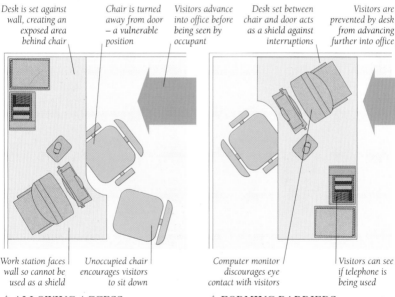

Desk is set against wall, creating an exposed area behind chair

Chair is turned away from door – a vulnerable position

Visitors advance into office before being seen by occupant

Desk set between chair and door acts as a shield against interruptions

Visitors are prevented by desk from advancing further into office

Work station faces wall so cannot be used as a shield

Unoccupied chair encourages visitors to sit down

Computer monitor discourages eye contact with visitors

Visitors can see if telephone is being used

▲ **ALLOWING ACCESS**
In this office you will be visible as soon as the door is opened. You are seated with your back to the door and have to turn to see who is coming in, making you unable to pre-empt unwelcome visitors.

▲ **FORMING BARRIERS**
Here, a computer forms a barrier between you and anyone entering the room. Your chair faces the door, so you can see approaching visitors. The lack of a spare chair will discourage visitors from staying too long.

FILTERING INFORMATION

Most people receive hundreds of different pieces of information every working day, and processing them takes up large amounts of time. Take time to work out a systematic way of handling all the incoming information that ends up on your desk.

49 Throw away any information that you think you do not need.

50 Keep all chance meetings short by standing – it will then be easier to get away.

GAINING INFORMATION

Information comes to you in increasingly diverse forms, including the following:

● On paper (for example, via post, faxes, memos, newspapers, magazines, journals, reports);

● Electronically (for example, via e-mail, intranet);

● By voice (for example, via face-to-face meetings, television, radio, telephone, voice mail).

Remember that some forms of information appear to be more urgent than others – but this may not be a true reflection of their importance. For example, phone calls often take precedence over post because they are more immediate.

PROCESSING INFORMATION

Try to establish a routine for processing set information. For example, if you know that the external post arrives at 10 a.m. and that internal messages are distributed at 11 a.m., set aside a time just before lunch for sorting through the mail. Read your electronic messages at the same time, and, if you have not already done so, make some time to skim newspapers and magazines.

You will need to repeat the same process towards the end of the day to tidy up your desk and to prepare yourself for the following morning. It is often a good idea to let information "stew" overnight before taking any action on it.

POINTS TO REMEMBER

● Messages arrive all the time and should not disrupt the work flow.

● Messages should be skim-read until their main information content is absorbed.

● If a message requires action, a note should be made and added to a master list.

● For ease of filing, a printed piece of information can be immediately coded with a folder name.

● Messages should be disposed of once they have been dealt with.

CIRCULATING MATERIAL

Much of the information that comes your way can be passed directly on to colleagues or staff. Divide information into three categories:

● That which you amend or add something to before passing on – this is typical of the general internal memo or report;
● That which you read, digest, then pass on to someone else – this is typically what happens with journals and magazines;
● That which you copy and distribute – you may do this with a thank-you letter from a happy, satisfied customer about which colleagues should be informed.

51 Copy information only to those who need to know.

52 Stop subscriptions to magazines you no longer read.

HANDLING DIFFERENT TYPES OF INFORMATION

INFORMATION SOURCES	HOW TO HANDLE THEM
INTERNAL MEMOS AND REPORTS Information contained in internal memos and reports can be specific to an individual, work team, department, committee, or other group.	● Timing is the critical element when circulating information of this type. ● Decide by when and for whom your comments or actions are needed. ● Plan to fit any action into your schedule.
EXTERNAL POST AND FAXES The range and importance of incoming information is very wide. Post is usually delivered at regular intervals, but faxes can arrive at any time.	● Decide what action is needed, and when. ● Ascertain whether you should distribute the information, and if so, in what form. ● Ensure that any information that needs filing is filed, and anything that is not needed is thrown away.
INTRANET AND E-MAIL Electronic messaging systems are being increasingly used for rapid communication and dissemination of information to individuals or groups.	● Electronic messages can be created and distributed easily, so check if they are relevant to you. ● Do not open messages that are not relevant to you. ● Once you have acted on a message or added it to your master list, delete it.
NEWSPAPERS AND MAGAZINES Much information on specific areas of a trade or profession can be sourced from a selective subscription list of newspapers and magazines.	● Skim-read articles and decide whether you want to keep them for future reference. ● Take a photocopy before passing a magazine on. ● Cut out information, mark relevant sections with red ink, and file in the appropriate place.

DEALING WITH REFERENCE

What should you do with material (both paper and electronic) that you want to read at a later date? One option is to keep it all in a separate "pending" file, and to dip in and out of the file as and when you have time for background reading. However, one of the problems with files such as these is that they have a tendency to become unmanageably large, so they need to be cleared out as regularly as possible. You should therefore try to clear the file of any outdated and irrelevant material each time you dip into it.

53 Remove magazine and newspaper articles you wish to keep, and file them for reference.

54 Keep only essential reading on your desk.

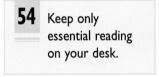

READING REFERENCE ▼
Read through relevant magazines and newspapers regularly to source up-to-date reference material. Build up a filing system to deal with this reading matter.

DELEGATING YOUR WORK

It is very daunting to return from time away, for example at meetings or on business travel, to find your desk covered in unprocessed messages and information. If you are often away from your desk, organize someone to filter these for you. The person to whom you delegate this responsibility should be able to sift through your messages and mail, distributing items to staff who can deal with them in your absence. Explain which matters can be handled at once and which are best saved for your return.

Useful articles can be torn from magazines for future reference

Reference and information can be stored in a reading file

KEEPING UP TO DATE

The relevance of information changes as time marches on. As most of today's news is history tomorrow, so our perspective of what is relevant alters over time. Some people believe that what is useless today may come in useful at a later date, and consequently tend to hoard all sorts of information. Generally, however, remember that it takes time and space to process written information, so always carefully consider the relevance of any reference material to your work before filing it away.

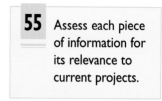

55 Assess each piece of information for its relevance to current projects.

PROCESSING INFORMATION

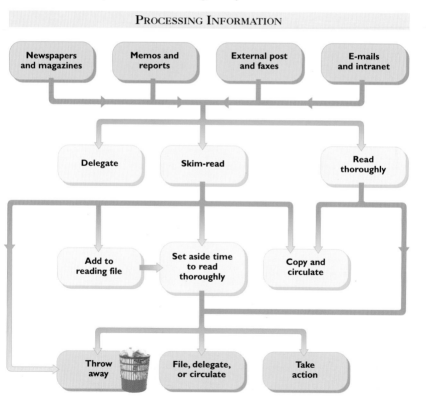

WORKING WITH OTHERS

The best-laid plans for managing time are always to some extent in the hands of others. Nobody works entirely alone. An unexpected telephone call can throw a day's plans into chaos. Learn to reconcile other people's time management with your own.

56 Think before you interrupt anyone. Their time is as valuable as yours.

QUESTIONS TO ASK YOURSELF

Q Do I consider others' plans when making my own?

Q Do I write too many unnecessary memos?

Q Do I organize too many rambling meetings?

Q Do I always arrive on time for appointments?

Q Do I frequently interrupt other people?

ASSESSING WORK ROLES

The extent to which you compromise your plans for somebody else depends on your relationship with that person. Consider, for example, whether you should call an urgent meeting that includes your boss, without discussing it first. Your boss may resent being involved in a meeting without prior consultation – perhaps he or she may have information that alters the agenda or makes the meeting unnecessary. It is essential always to think through the decisions you make when dealing with colleagues at all levels of seniority.

REVIEWING YOUR ASSUMPTIONS

Many people make erroneous judgments about what constitutes good management of time – it is easy to confuse someone seeming to be busy with them working hard and managing their time well. When working with others, analyze their work practices before making assumptions about their productivity. Consider whether you could save time by adapting your work methods to mirror theirs, or vice versa.

My colleagues spend too much time discussing rather than working

My colleagues do not work long enough hours

My colleagues waste time and money on lunches

My colleagues are not busy enough

My colleagues take too many days off

▲ MAKING FALSE ASSUMPTIONS

If you are guilty of looking at your workmates and making false assumptions about how they manage their time, rethink your attitude. Are they really being unproductive, or do they achieve results from spending time in meetings, discussions, and lunches?

ANALYZING MOTIVATION

Everyone is motivated by different aspects of their job. If you think your workmates could make better use of their time, consider whether they are demotivated. This could be because:

- They do not get enough work to do – in which case, redistribute work around the department to ensure everyone has busy schedule;
- They feel frustrated because they are not interested in the work they are doing – discuss a more fulfilling programme of work;
- They feel overworked – help them to develop their time-management skills or consider whether they can reduce their workload.

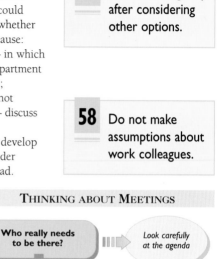

57 Call a meeting only after considering other options.

58 Do not make assumptions about work colleagues.

HANDLING MEETINGS

You work with others most often when attending meetings. Organizing a meeting between busy people can be complex and time-consuming. It takes time to set up, prepare an agenda, travel to and from a meeting, and follow-up. On top of which, meetings take up time that participants could spend on other activities. Always ask yourself if it is really necessary to bring people together. You might be able to save time by not calling a meeting, but instead speaking to individuals by phone, for example. If all the participants work for the same organization, it will be to your mutual benefit if time spent in meetings is kept to a minimum.

THINKING ABOUT MEETINGS

Who really needs to be there? → *Look carefully at the agenda*

Should everybody be there all the time? → *Allow for people to come and go*

Will people need to travel? → *Consider other options*

Can the meeting deal with other business? → *Make the most of the situation*

Can the meeting be cancelled? → *Resolve matters without the meeting*

MAKING PHONE CALLS

There is hardly a business in existence that does not depend on the phone and, increasingly, voice mail for rapid and direct communications. Their effective and appropriate use can dramatically improve your efficiency and performance.

59 Take a deep, relaxing breath before you make a phone call.

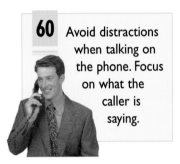

60 Avoid distractions when talking on the phone. Focus on what the caller is saying.

CHOOSING WHEN TO CALL

Set aside a specific time of day for making phone calls, and list all the calls that you need to make every day. Be clear about the purpose of each call, and draw up a brief agenda for each as if the call was a meeting. Then make sure that you cover all the items on the agenda during the conversation. Prioritize your calls in order of importance, to ensure that you concentrate your time and resources on the most important and urgent calls.

KEEPING ON TRACK

Do not let a phone conversation stray too far from your agenda unless there is a good reason, such as dealing with an unexpected problem. Take notes, and tick off items on your agenda as they are covered. You may find it easier to lead your conversation if you stand up or walk about.

It is easy to lose track of time when speaking to someone whose conversation you enjoy, but try to keep this in check. Assess the purpose of the call – for example, can you be brief or do you need to spend time building up a rapport or placating an angry customer? As an exercise, use a timer for a week to monitor the length of time you spend on each call. This can be sobering, both because of both the cost of the call itself and the cost in terms of your time.

THINGS TO DO

1. Prepare yourself for a phone conversation as you would for a meeting.

2. Bunch calls together. If a number is engaged, try it after completing other calls.

3. Choose an order of priority in which to make your calls.

4. Use a speaker phone so that you can do other work while waiting for an answer.

5. If you use a pager, put aside time to return all your calls.

USING A VOICE MAIL SYSTEM

Corporate answering machines, also known as voice mail, are becoming commonplace. Some people dislike the impersonal nature of voice mail, but you need to understand how the system works and how to make efficient use of it. It is an ideal tool for arranging internal meetings or eliciting a response from a busy colleague. Avoid bargaining or making deals by means of a seemingly endless series of voice-mail messages, since you need to speak directly to customers or suppliers to gauge reactions and find areas of compromise and agreement.

61 When making a phone call, have another project to hand to work on in case you are kept waiting.

DO'S AND DON'TS

✔ Do introduce yourself. "This is Brian Smith. I'm ringing about...".

✔ Do be aware of the amount of time you spend on each call.

✔ Do be clear about the points you want to discuss every time you make a call.

✔ Do leave short, concise messages on answer machines.

✘ Don't start a call with "Hello" and expect to be recognized.

✘ Don't put off urgent, difficult calls to deal with easier and less important ones.

✘ Don't continue a call if you have a bad line. Hang up and call back.

✘ Don't make important calls unless you are fully prepared.

CHOOSING A TELEPHONE TO SUIT YOUR NEEDS

Telephones now have a tremendous range of optional extras; look into the choices to see whether they can be used to help you work any more efficiently. Facilities available include call diversion, fast-dialling buttons, desk speakers, conference lines, and small screens that show an incoming caller's number and name before you pick up the receiver. There is no point, however, in having a host of buttons and features that you do not use. Choose a telephone system with features that you actually do need.

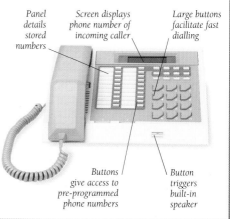

Panel details stored numbers

Screen displays phone number of incoming caller

Large buttons facilitate fast dialling

Buttons give access to pre-programmed phone numbers

Button triggers built-in speaker

TAKING PHONE CALLS

Receiving phone calls is very different from making calls. Incoming calls can take you by surprise and interrupt you when you are unprepared. Develop techniques to reduce the time wasted and enable you to deal with callers when you choose to do so.

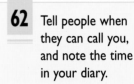

62 Tell people when they can call you, and note the time in your diary.

MAKING TIME FOR CALLS

Phone callers have the upper hand in deciding when they want to make a call, but modern technology is shifting the balance of power between caller and called. To some extent you can now dictate the time when you receive calls, enabling you to arrange your working day as you prefer. If you have an answer machine or voice-mail system, leave a short message on it saying when you will be in your office, and that callers should ring back at that time. If you have a secretary, route all your calls via him or her, with instructions regarding to whom you wish to speak and when it would be most convenient.

SIGNALLING THE END OF A PHONE CALL

It can be difficult to end a phone conversation initiated by somebody else, but do not assume that it is up to them to close. If you are too busy to talk, tell the caller just that, and explain your reasons politely. Try one of the following phrases:

❝ *Is there anything else we need to discuss before I go?* ❞

❝ *I have got a call on my other line. Is it okay to call you back another time?* ❞

❝ *Perhaps we can discuss this further next time we speak.* ❞

❝ *I must go. My boss is signalling at me to join her from the other end of the room.* ❞

DEALING WITH COLD CALLERS

If you have secretarial staff, brief them not to transfer cold callers through to you. If a persistent caller does succeed in getting through, politely but firmly inform him or her that you are not interested in what they are offering. Remember that, however annoying it may be to have interruptions from cold callers, they are only doing their job and you should always treat them courteously.

DO'S AND DON'TS

✔ Do be polite.

✔ Do keep an open mind. Cold callers may have information that is useful to you.

✔ Do suggest someone who may be interested in the product or proposal being offered.

✔ Do get a phone that shows a caller's number as they ring. If you do not know the number, you need not take the call.

✘ Don't ask cold callers to call back. They will, and it may be at a less convenient time.

✘ Don't say you will call back if you have no intention of doing so.

✘ Don't ask a caller to send details unless you are genuinely interested.

✘ Don't answer questions with long rambling sentences. Keep to the point.

RECORDING MESSAGES

Use a recorded message on your answer phone or voice-mail system to influence the replies you receive. A crisp, brief message invites a crisp, brief reply. If your machine allows you to limit the lengths of incoming messages, use this feature to force callers to leave short messages. Messages will then take you less time to listen to, and this will free your time. Set aside a convenient time each day to play back and make a note of all your messages.

63 Reroute your calls when you want to avoid interruptions.

▼ NOTING MESSAGES
Play back your messages, noting any action required. Add these tasks to your master list.

READING AND WRITING

Many people spend a significant proportion of their working lives reading and absorbing information, as well as providing it in the form of memos, letters, and reports. Learn how to cope with these well, and you will save a great deal of time.

64 Never delay dealing with any written material – it will just mount up.

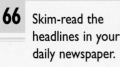

65 Underline key phrases in reports you have to read.

66 Skim-read the headlines in your daily newspaper.

LEARNING TO SKIM-READ

Everybody wastes time reading sentences that link the important points made in text. Learn to skim-read from paragraph to paragraph, identifying the key words in each. Effective skim-reading requires practice. Start with a piece of text, and read every word. As you go along, underline one key word in each paragraph, then go back over the text and see if you can reconstruct the sense from the key words you have chosen. Repeat on new pieces of text until eventually you can identify key words quickly and easily.

ASSESSING MATERIAL

When reading reports and articles, try to get an overview of their contents first. Read any introduction or summary, and take time to look at the list of contents. If you have a long report to read, start by glancing through it from beginning to end, noting the headings and the lengths of different sections. When you read the report in full – either immediately or later on – you will then find you have a good idea of its content and structure, helping you to read it quickly and efficiently. The same also applies to newspapers and magazines. If you do not have enough time to read your daily paper, make a mental note of the main headlines, and skim the digest section.

POINTS TO REMEMBER

- The main purpose when reading is to understand the material.
- Not everything can be understood fully after one read. It takes time to absorb a long list of points, so relevant documents must always be read carefully.
- Skim-reading is generally suitable for documents such as memos; not for more detailed material.
- Readers need to be led through a report, so directional signposts should be included.
- A document should always be written with the reader in mind.

COPING WITH WRITER'S BLOCK

If you have trouble starting to write, vary your approach until you find the system that works for you. A report does not have to be written in its final order, and may be less daunting if you divide it into small sections. Introductions and conclusions can be difficult, so try starting wherever inspiration strikes – the important thing is to get something down in writing from which to work. It is often easiest to "top and tail" a report after writing the main text.

DO'S AND DON'TS

✔ Do prepare an outline before you write.

✔ Do read your work as if it is new to you.

✔ Do keep in mind the point you are making while you write, and use clear language.

✘ Don't stare at a blank computer screen – write anything.

✘ Don't make your text too complex or too simple for your reader.

✘ Don't pad your work with irrelevant facts.

◀ FACING A BLANK SCREEN

Even experienced writers are sometimes lost for words. Instead of staring blankly at a screen, try writing the first thing that comes into your head – you may find that this unblocks your thoughts and allows your ideas to flow more freely.

CUTTING OUT PAPERWORK

To cut down on the amount of writing you have to do, learn to deal effectively with incoming correspondence such as memos and faxes. Your response may merit a lengthy reply, but it may be more appropriate to add a quick, handwritten note on the original before passing it on; this is much quicker, and saves on paper. Delegate the opening of your mail to your assistant or a junior member of your team. Brief them about what they can deal with themselves, and how to prioritize items for your attention. This way you can reduce the volume of paper that you handle yourself.

67 Keep essential reference material separate from your other documents and papers.

USING TECHNOLOGY

Few people today can make effective use of their time if they do not understand the basics of information technology (IT) – the convergence of telecommunications and computing. IT puts libraries in our offices and a postal service at our beck and call.

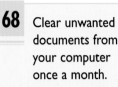

68 Clear unwanted documents from your computer once a month.

69 Consider carefully your computing requirements.

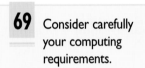

▼ STORING INFORMATION
Keep your documents and folders well organized. If you do not, the desktop will become a mess of icons labelled with names that no longer mean anything to you. Take half an hour each month to go through your computer, keeping folders up to date and deleting things you no longer need.

FILING ON A COMPUTER

Design a system for storing information along the same lines as a filing system for paperwork. Create a method of classification that suits your business, and label your documents clearly and logically. Keep your data in documents stored in folders on a hard disk (the computer's memory) or on removable floppy disks (the equivalent of a series of filing cabinets). Electronic data can be corrupted by magnetic fields, and an electricity surge can result in the loss of data on a hard or floppy disk, so make a back-up copy of important material on a separate disk, and label it clearly.

BEFORE FILING

AFTER FILING — *Folder is labelled clearly*

budgets

letters

Randomly located document can accidentally be deleted

Folder is unlabelled

All related documents are grouped together in one folder

USING E-MAIL

There are two types of e-mail system: intranets within companies, used mainly to relay messages between colleagues, and Internet-based e-mail, which allows for international communication. E-mail is easy to use and can be a channel for more than just simple messages. You can send any document on a computer as an attachment to an e-mail, so you will not need to import or retype, as long as the recipient has the right software to read it. Because of its immediacy, e-mail is an informal medium and strict rules of grammar and formal written language tend not to be used. But remember that confidentiality is not guaranteed.

70 Keep your e-mail messages short, and address them accurately.

SEARCHING ON THE INTERNET

The Internet has a number of search engines – systems that enable you to search for information speedily. To ensure a successful search, carefully choose the keywords for which you ask the search engine to look. If you do not, you will be given an unmanageable number of references, many of which will not be relevant. If your choice is too narrow, the search engine may not find anything.

Internet address of Web-site page currently accessed

Icon for searching Internet

Icon for accessing e-mail service

USING A ▶ WEB-SITE PAGE

In Internet language, a Web page is what you see on a computer screen. A Web site may be elaborate and contain many pages, and will usually provide links to many other related sites.

Underlined keywords indicating links with other pages

Status bar indicating page downloading time

HOLDING MEETINGS

Meetings consume a large proportion of the average working week. Typically, a manager spends up to half of each week in meetings. Making sure that meetings run smoothly and achieve their purpose is an essential ingredient of time management.

71 Encourage people to express views, even if they are contrary to yours.

MEETING ONE TO ONE

One-to-one meetings are more flexible than large, formal gatherings, and their duration is more easily controlled. Nevertheless, you need to achieve a delicate balance between cutting a meeting too short, leaving the other person feeling frustrated, and allowing it to go on so long that both parties feel their time is being wasted.

72 Keep meetings short by listening rather than talking.

ASSESSING STAFF ▼
Staff assessments are a sensitive example of one-to-one meetings. They should be of fixed duration and free from interruption to allow frank communication.

Manager talks encouragingly and directly

Subordinate responds in receptive and confident manner

Subordinate notes key points

TIMING SMALL MEETINGS

Some one-to-one meetings have a very specific purpose, such as recruitment or staff assessment, and in these cases there usually tends to be a well-understood format and duration. Less formal one-to-one meetings tend to be either short and focused, in response to a particular situation (such as a reprimand), or more general and of indefinite duration. In these latter cases, avoid unnecessary time-wasting for both parties by deciding informally on an agenda and time frame for the meeting beforehand. Be disciplined in adhering to it. This way, both parties' expectations of the meeting's purpose will be clarified, minimizing the need to spend time resolving misunderstandings afterwards.

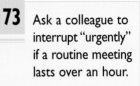

73 Ask a colleague to interrupt "urgently" if a routine meeting lasts over an hour.

▼ REPRIMANDING STAFF

Reprimands should be brief, without anger, and as close as possible to the offending event; try to ensure that the issue is dealt with and resolved in a single meeting. Use assertive body language to emphasize and reinforce your message.

Subordinate's head is tilted downwards, but he maintains eye contact with manager

Manager assumes dominant position by standing and leaning across desk

PLANNING LARGE MEETINGS

Make sure that everybody attending a meeting knows, in advance, its purpose and their role. Circulate an agenda well beforehand to tell participants which subjects are to be discussed. This will allow them to prepare any necessary information and gain an idea of the duration of the meeting. It will be easier for the chairperson to control time-wasting tactics if everybody is aware that the agenda must be covered within the set time limit. Your agenda will also help to define the amount of time allocated to individual items.

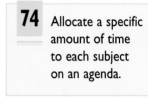

74 Allocate a specific amount of time to each subject on an agenda.

75 Encourage people to attend only the parts of a meeting that concern them.

CULTURAL DIFFERENCES

Different cultures view meetings in different ways, so the handling of a meeting depends to some extent on the nationalities of those present. The Japanese consider it an insult if you appear alone at a meeting – they honour their hosts by appearing in numbers. In Arab countries, it is not usual to be told how long a meeting will last. It will finish when all the guests are ready to leave.

PREPARING AN AGENDA

The order in which items appear on an agenda can have a powerful effect on a meeting's timing. Avoid heading an agenda with a contentious subject, since the participants in the meeting may spend too much time discussing it instead of moving on to the next item. Instead, begin with routine and straightforward business, which offers easy decisions. This gives the meeting a feeling of achievement and the impetus to progress rapidly.

AVOIDING TIME-WASTING

Time-wasting in meetings costs more than just the participants' time; the monetary cost of a meeting may be considerable when the combined salaries of those present are taken into account. So it is imperative that time is not lost by people attending unnecessary meetings, by meetings being disrupted, or by meetings failing to achieve their objectives. Do not tolerate tactics such as lengthy, irrelevant speeches by fellow participants, or the endless revising of points. If you are the chairperson, it will be your role to recognize such tactics and ensure that the meeting is kept moving.

KEEPING TO SCHEDULE

Meetings should start punctually: begin without latecomers, and do not waste time recapping for them when they arrrive. Keep a careful track of time throughout a meeting to ensure the agenda is covered in the allotted time. In general, defer overrunning items until the end of the meeting so that other items can be dealt with on schedule.

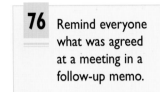

76 Remind everyone what was agreed at a meeting in a follow-up memo.

KEEPING A MEETING ON COURSE

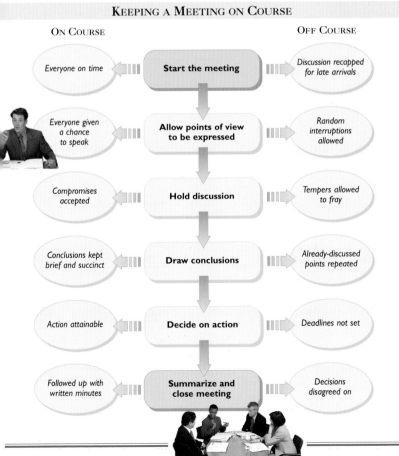

ON COURSE		OFF COURSE
Everyone on time	**Start the meeting**	Discussion recapped for late arrivals
Everyone given a chance to speak	**Allow points of view to be expressed**	Random interruptions allowed
Compromises accepted	**Hold discussion**	Tempers allowed to fray
Conclusions kept brief and succinct	**Draw conclusions**	Already-discussed points repeated
Action attainable	**Decide on action**	Deadlines not set
Followed up with written minutes	**Summarize and close meeting**	Decisions disagreed on

TRAVELLING FOR WORK

With the development of the global marketplace, a growing number of people are finding that travel is an integral part of their job. Organizing business trips effectively is now an essential part of time management for many managers.

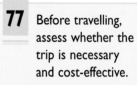

77 Before travelling, assess whether the trip is necessary and cost-effective.

78 If possible, fit everything you need to take into one small piece of hand luggage.

ASSESSING NEED

Before making plans to travel, ask yourself a number of questions about the trip. Am I making the best use of my time by going on this trip? Will a phone call or letter suffice instead? Can I send someone else? Can I persuade the people I need to see to come to me? Can I meet them half way? If the answer to any of these is yes, seriously question the time-effectiveness of your trip.

PACKING EFFICIENTLY

Effective packing requires you to make an accurate assessment of your needs based on the duration of your trip. For a short trip, take just enough clothing and accessories with you to cover the number of days you anticipate being away. This way you do not have to spend money on laundry services. However, if you are going to be away for more than a few days, it may be better to take only one or two changes of clothes and have them cleaned on the trip, rather than burdening yourself with heavy suitcases.

79 Take work to do in an airport lounge in case of delays.

▼ **PACKING A BRIEFCASE**
Be selective about what you take. Assess what documents and equipment you will need for any meetings you have planned and for staying in touch with your office.

Background material

Mobile phone eases contact with office

Diary contains detailed travel itinerary

Files necessary for trip

MANAGING YOUR TRAVEL TIME

BEFORE YOU TRAVEL

- Carefully plan your route and itinerary.
- Combine numerous visits within the same country or region if possible.
- Draw up a precise daily schedule. Leave a copy with colleagues at the office so that you can be contacted if necessary.
- Gather together all the documents you will need for your meetings while you are away.
- Always confirm arrangements before you set out in case a meeting needs to be rescheduled or is no longer necessary.
- Prepare a permanent general file containing essential information that you can use each time you visit a particular area.
- Reserve seats in advance when travelling by train so that you can avoid queuing and arrive at the station just before the train departs.

WHILE YOU ARE AWAY

- Keep in touch with your office so that you can update them on your progress and keep abreast of any new developments that will affect your plans.
- Use a dictaphone for memos or notes, or a laptop for e-mails or other work that can be done on-screen.
- Use your own alarm clock as a back-up in case the early-morning alarm calls in your hotel prove to be unreliable.
- At your destination, travel at off-peak times if possible; it is less stressful – and may be quicker – than battling through the rush-hour commuters.
- Combine meals with business meetings to save time and create a more informal and congenial working atmosphere.

COPING WITH JET-LAG

Your daily life is governed by an internal body clock which regulates sleep patterns. Jet-lag occurs when you travel through different time zones and disrupt this clock. If you are travelling to a time zone with a 2- or 3- hour difference from your own, try going to bed when it is time to sleep at your destination on the day before you travel. This allows your body to adopt the new sleep pattern. For places with a larger time difference, ensure you are well rested before you travel and allow rest time upon arrival.

◀ **TRAVEL LIGHT**
Today's bags and suitcases are better designed and more ergonomic than ever before. Use a trolley bag with wheels to save lifting a heavy case. Carry a suit carrier and small trolley bag on to a plane as hand luggage to save time on arrival at your destination.

Hard-cased trolley bag

Suit carrier

80 Set your watch to the local time at your destination.

STAYING IN TOUCH

While it is important to work out how you are going to keep in touch with your office when travelling, try to be realistic about it. There are many methods of communication you can use, with varying levels of complexity. Choose the method best suited to your needs. In some situations, your absence from work may cause practical difficulties. For example, your signature may be required to validate important documents. In such circumstances, it may be appropriate to book an overnight courier to get the documents to you and to take them back to the office.

POINTS TO REMEMBER

● A fax is faster than a mailed letter and often cheaper.

● Modems can be attached to portable computers, enabling you to send faxes or e-mail.

● Mobile telephones do not work in all parts of some countries.

● International call costs can vary, so options such as telephone bureaux and kiosks should always be checked before any telephone calls are made from overseas.

COMMUNICATING WHILE TRAVELLING

Communicating with colleagues at your office while on a business trip is now more convenient and reliable than ever. Use any one of the following methods according to your location and the type of communication you want to send or receive.

MOBILE ▶ PHONE
Most mobile phones now offer overseas communications. They are useful in areas where there are no public telephones.

▲ TELEPHONE
Leave a contact number with your office. Note that most hotels charge large premiums to use the phones in the rooms.

▲ FAX MACHINE
Send messages by fax if you want a fast reply. Some hotels have machines in their rooms or a central fax in reception.

◀ E-MAIL
Send documents and communications that need instant attention by e-mail. To access e-mail you will need a computer set up with a modem link.

◀ MAIL
Use guaranteed delivery services for sending original documents or those that require a signature. Air-mail can be used for less urgent items.

KEEPING ON TOP OF WORK

Before you travel, draw up a schedule that utilizes your time to the optimum; this will minimize the time you are away and reduce the cost of the trip. Many people think that they can carry on with their normal job while on a business trip, but this is not possible in the majority of cases – nor is it always necessary. Ensure that your business trip has a specific purpose and keep free time to a minimum. Use any time you have available to concentrate on the purpose of your trip.

81 Check how much your hotel charges for phone calls before making any.

UPDATING YOUR NOTES

82 Find out whether you need adapters for your electrical equipment abroad.

Most of your time on business trips will be spent attending meetings; the longer the trip the more meetings you will attend. It is crucial to update your notes every day, otherwise all your meetings will have merged into each other by the time you return to your office; you will not be able to recall who agreed to what and when. Allow time each day to write up the day's meetings, noting any decisions made and action to be taken.

◀ **WORKING IN YOUR ROOM**
Take advantage of the peace and quiet of a hotel room to write up the day's events and prepare for the next day's meetings. Use a laptop computer to record the proceedings and results of your meetings and correspond with your office. As an alternative, have the details of your your meetings typed up and sent back to your office electronically by hotel business centre staff.

SCHEDULING TIME OFF

Managing your time successfully involves more than just organizing your workload. Work will suffer if you do not schedule regular breaks to recharge your batteries. Try to make time for family and friends, hobbies, and leisure activities.

83 Take two or three short holidays each year instead of one long one.

POINTS TO REMEMBER

- Taking time off should not make you feel guilty. It will help you to be more effective in your work.

- Even a few minutes' break from work can be rejuvenating.

- A working holiday is a complete contradiction in terms.

- Exercise helps to reduce stress and can provide a useful break from work if your workplace has showers and changing facilities.

- Holidays and time off work should be regarded as a good exercise in delegation.

TAKING DAILY BREAKS

Some business leaders include a regular period in their day when they briefly take time off. Similar to the siesta, it is often taken after lunch. Their doors are shut to interruptions, allowing them to take a short period of semi-sleep (only about 10 minutes), which has a recuperative effect on the body. Schedule a set time each day to switch off; pick a quiet period that fits in with your personal energy rhythm and work obligations. With practice, you will be able to reduce this rest time.

It can be difficult to find a suitable place to take such a break. Open plan offices lack privacy and are noisy, making it difficult to relax. Try to find a vacant room or office away from all disturbances.

84 Schedule regular time off to pursue your hobbies and leisure interests.

◀ TAKING TIME FOR YOURSELF

Do not rush straight back to work after a hectic meeting – take a break in a café, or go for a walk. Time out will allow you to clear your head and restore your energy.

RECHARGING BATTERIES

To recharge your batteries you must lead a well-balanced life and schedule time off. Spend this time with family and friends, exercise regularly, eat properly, learn new things, and take holidays. If you do not have school-age children, plan breaks to coincide with quiet periods at work. Off-season holidays can also provide relaxation, since destinations are less crowded.

▲ **GETTING AWAY**
A change of scene can provide a breathing space from work and help you to relax. Holidaying with your family or friends allows you to take a break from the pressures of your daily routine and work-related stress. Even a short break away can be beneficial.

PLANNING AHEAD

Good time management means planning ahead. Scheduling holidays in advance allows you to organize your workload around your breaks. At the start of each year, take the time and effort to organize your diary. Work out when you are likely to be busy and when your workload will be lightest. Look ahead at the year as a whole, and plan your holidays accordingly. Ask everybody in your office to do the same with their own schedules, and you will soon be able to see if any conflicts of time are going to arise.

85 Aim to experience something new every day.

▼ **ORGANIZING TIME OFF**
Estimate the time needed to complete your work commitments over the year, and block it out on a wall chart. You will then be able to assess the best times to take holidays.

JAN	FEB	MAR	APR	MAY	JUN	JUL	AUG	SEPT	OCT	NOV	DEC

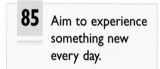

■ *Time allocated for regular work events*

■ *Time allocated to deal with heavy workload*

■ *Time allocated for breaks due to light workload*

MANAGING THE TIME OF OTHERS

To make the best use of your time, you also have to manage that of your staff, colleagues, and seniors. Learn to delegate well, share tasks, and manage upwards as well as down.

COMMUNICATING WELL

To manage others so that you all make the best use of available time, you first need to master the art of communication. This is not just a matter of deciding what your message is; it is also about deciding how to communicate that message.

86 Maintain high expectations, and people will live up to them.

CULTURAL DIFFERENCES

Hierarchy is deeply embedded in the cultures of most Eastern countries, and age still matters. If you are a young manager, do not expect to be listened to in China, for instance. Deference will be awarded to a consultant with grey hair, even if you both give exactly the same message.

SPREADING INFORMATION

Today, companies are evolving in a way that makes it easier for the people within them to communicate with each other. A gradual cultural change has meant that organizations are more open. You can use this new openness to save time, for example by spreading information verbally rather than writing a memo. Spoken communication has the added advantage of being two-way, encouraging the involvement of staff and allowing refinement of detail. But any important points covered verbally should also be noted in writing to minimize later uncertainties.

REVISING METHODS

Intranets and e-mail systems allow rapid, widespread dissemination of information. They can also make working at home without losing touch with colleagues a more practical and attractive option than it used to be. However, beware of information overload: the volume of data may make what is effectively junk e-mail seem more important than it is, and the ease of electronic communication can make it tempting to send messages that are not strictly necessary. Remember, too, that as organizations become less hierarchical and lines of communication open out, recipients may lack necessary background information, so always be clear and precise to avoid time-wasting misunderstandings.

87 Persuade others of your case using facts, not emotions.

88 Take an interest in what others are trying to achieve.

◀ ANALYZING INFORMATION FLOW
Certain communication lines in any organization are better developed than others. For instance, sales staff spend more time in contact with the production department than with colleagues in administration.

KEY

◀▬▶ *Communicates frequently*

◀▬▶ *Communicates occasionally*

◀▬▶ *Communicates rarely*

89 Hearing is not the same as listening. Learn to listen.

SALES DIRECTOR

ACCOUNTS MANAGER

PRODUCTION MANAGER

SALES MANAGER

ACCOUNTS ASSISTANT

PRODUCTION ASSISTANT

SALES REPRESENTATIVE

DELEGATING EFFECTIVELY

One of the keys to effective management is delegating work to others – no one can do everything for themselves. Learn to delegate aspects of your work properly, and you will have time to complete the most important elements of your job successfully.

90 Make sure you define objectives clearly when you delegate a task.

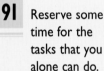

91 Reserve some time for the tasks that you alone can do.

POINTS TO REMEMBER

- When you delegate, you are not delegating the right to perform an action, you are delegating the right to make decisions.
- It is important to be flexible, as the person to whom you delegate may have a better and faster way of completing a job than you.
- A brief can be misinterpreted, so it is a good idea to ask for it to be repeated back to you.
- Overall responsibility for a delegated task remains with you.
- It is helpful to others if you can provide constructive feedback on their performance.
- Too much criticism is far more harmful than too much praise.

LEARNING TO DELEGATE

The process of delegation comprises the decision to delegate, the briefing, and the follow-up. At each of these points, anticipate the potential problems.

- The decision: persuade yourself to delegate. You will not benefit if you work to the assumption that it takes longer to teach somebody else to do a job than to do it yourself. Delegation has its own rewards – once someone has learned a particular task, they will be able to do it in the future without repeated briefings. However, be sure to delegate each job to a person with the appropriate skills and knowledge.
- The briefing: make sure that the person to whom you are delegating clearly understands the brief – what you want them to do and by when. Offer ongoing support and guidance.
- The follow-up: during the course of the project, check the standard of work produced. Provide positive feedback, but beware of overdoing it – there is a narrow line between helpful supervision and debilitating interference.

92 Keep a checklist to help you monitor the progress of tasks that you have delegated to others.

REINFORCING A BRIEF

In addition to providing a clear brief when delegating, you must provide all the information necessary for someone to complete the task successfully. To avoid any misinterpretation of the facts, take time to explain exactly what you expect, and how the project fits into your overall plan. Discuss any difficulties that may occur and how they could be tackled, and answer queries as they arise during completion of the task.

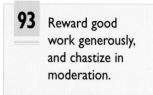

93 Reward good work generously, and chastize in moderation.

STRENGTHENING RESPONSIBILITY

94 Set precise and realistic deadlines for tasks that you delegate.

Delegation does not mean handing over control of a project, but handing over responsibility for certain tasks. Encourage individuals to work using their own methods, providing they stick to the brief. This allows you to exploit their specialized knowledge, or to provide them with an opportunity to develop a new area of expertise. One of the common contentions arising out of delegation is conflict over responsibility, so it is vital to define exactly what the delegate is responsible for.

DELEGATING CHOICES

Someone who has done similar work ⇐ **Delegate to whom?** ⇒ A novice

By memo, fax, or e-mail ⇐ **How to brief?** ⇒ By meeting face-to-face

As and when needed ⇐ **How to check progress?** ⇒ Daily

MANAGING COLLEAGUES

One of the most difficult things to get right is managing interruptions from colleagues. Either you become too available to each other, in which case you lose control of your time, or you are too distant and fail to take advantage of each other's abilities.

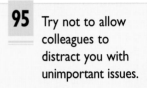

95 Try not to allow colleagues to distract you with unimportant issues.

WORKING TOGETHER

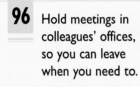

96 Hold meetings in colleagues' offices, so you can leave when you need to.

Traditional corporate hierarchies are gradually being flattened, and more tasks are now being assigned to teams designed and brought together for one-off projects. This means that you need to be able to work side-by-side with a variety of individuals and find ways of agreeing with them about work priorities and time management.

SHARING YOUR TIME-MANAGEMENT SKILLS

TASKS	WAYS TO SHARE SKILLS
PRIORITIZING WORK	● Talk through the principles of dividing work into A-, B-, and C-tasks and allocating a set number of each to do every day. ● Use examples from your colleagues' workload.
USING DIARIES AND PLANNERS	● Ask your colleagues to keep a time log, then review and analyze it with them to discover their various working patterns. ● Help your colleagues to set up an appropriate planning system.
FILTERING INFORMATION	● Encourage your colleagues to assess every item of information they receive to decide what action is required. ● Provide hints on faster reading based on your own experience.
DELEGATING AND FOLLOWING UP	● Discuss specific, related examples from the past to determine the best course of action in this instance. ● Be prepared to review any new systems that are set up.

FOCUSING ON OBJECTIVES

A good time-saving habit for you and your colleagues to get into is always to ask yourselves what you expect when you meet to discuss an issue. There is a useful mnemonic – AID – that helps in classifying the options available to you. Is it Advice you need from each other, is it Information, or is it a Decision? At the beginning of each discussion, indicate exactly what you are looking for from each other and you will all be more aware of the demands that the exchange will make on your time. You can also use the AID technique to help you to decide how to respond to colleagues seeking your attention.

USING AID OPTIONS

ADVICE
If you are going to give advice to a colleague, make sure that you do it when you have plenty of time available. It is best to give advice only when you are not in a hurry.

INFORMATION
Dispensing information is a one-way process – in most cases it does not require any feedback. Set aside a short amount of time in your day for giving out information.

DECISION
Reaching a decision may well take some considerable time. It is important that you do not allow yourself to be hurried into an over-hasty decision by an anxious colleague.

ENCOURAGING OPINIONS

The unique thing about most colleagues is that they can give you dispassionate, on-the-job feedback, which you often cannot get from further up or lower down the organizational hierarchy. Unlike colleagues, seniors and subordinates may think too much in terms of job assessments.

Encourage your colleagues to give you their opinions of your performance. They may raise some helpful points that will save you time in the future. For example, they may let you know that your meetings last too long or are disorganized, or that you appear to be inaccessible to others when they need you. Listen to their advice, and adopt any useful time-saving techniques.

97 Set aside special times when your office is open to all.

98 Visit colleagues only when you have more than one issue to discuss.

MANAGING YOUR MANAGER

Everyone should know how to manage their managers if they want to be able to make the best possible use of their own time. Learn to do this discreetly so that your seniors do not feel as though they are being undermined or manipulated.

99 Be aware of your boss's working patterns, and try to adapt to them.

100 Ask about your boss's home life – it will help to build up a relationship.

BUILDING A RELATIONSHIP

The first thing you need to know is exactly what your manager expects of you. Do you have the sort of manager who delegates a task to you and then gives you the freedom to get on with it, or are you expected to report back every day and to wait around until they are free to hear you? Discuss this matter tactfully with your manager early on. That way you can tailor the way you work to fit in with your boss's expectations.

If you decide you would like more autonomy, persuade your seniors to trust you by establishing a strong relationship with them. When you have a good relationship with your manager, you can be less formal, and communication becomes easier, more direct, and therefore more efficient.

Bring more than one thing at a time to discuss with your boss

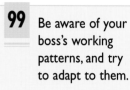

◀ SORTING OUT QUERIES
Take the initiative and arrange a time to see your manager, rather than waiting for your manager to come to see you. They may be so involved with their work that they do not realize that you need help from time to time.

COMMUNICATING EFFICIENTLY

In any relationship with your seniors, there is an implicit assumption that they are busier than you, and that the claims on their time are more pressing than the claims on yours. When you have something to discuss, make your communication brief. Get to the point quickly, and try to anticipate any queries that your seniors may raise. Keep your conversations high on factual content and low on your personal opinions.

DO'S AND DON'TS

✔ Do arrive at meetings well prepared and with any relevant documentation.

✔ Do take relevant notes, and give your boss a copy.

✔ Do gather together queries to avoid constantly interrupting your manager.

✔ Do work out whether your manager prefers written or spoken information, and supply it in that way.

✘ Don't volunteer your opinions unless they are requested or you feel they are important or relevant.

✘ Don't present any problems without offering some viable solutions to them.

✘ Don't be late for meetings with your manager.

✘ Don't mistake your boss's occasional thoughtless action for maliciousness.

GETTING YOUR OWN WAY

As you build up a personal relationship with your manager, you will learn what it takes to get your own way – and thus work more efficiently and with a greater amount of satisfaction. Of course, the priorities of your manager will alter all the time (as will your own), and it is your job to keep abreast of those changes and adapt sensitively to fluctuating demands. Remember that there is little to be gained in being abrasive towards your seniors. This will simply irritate them, making them feel defensive, less willing to listen to you, and unsympathetic to your viewpoint. Try to be aware of the pressures that your manager is under, and be sympathetic.

KNOWING WHEN TO OFFER ADVICE

It is a useful tool to think of communication with your manager in terms of the AID acronym: Advice, Information, and Decision. Offer your boss advice either when it is asked for, or when you feel it would be welcomed. However, you should give relevant or important information without constraint. It is often possible to influence your boss to make a different decision to the one he or she was going to make. Remember, though, that there may be reasons behind a decision of which you are unaware.

| 101 | Remember that time is perfectly democratic. Nobody has more or less of it than you. |

INDEX

ACKNOWLEDGMENTS

AUTHOR'S ACKNOWLEDGMENTS

The production of this book has called on the skills of many people. I would like particularly to mention my editors at Dorling Kindersley, and my assistant Jane Williams.

PUBLISHER'S ACKNOWLEDGMENTS

Dorling Kindersley would like to thank Emma Lawson for her valuable part in the planning and development of this series, everyone who generously lent props for the photoshoots, and the following for their help and participation:

Editorial Tracey Beresford, Marian Broderick, Anna Cheifetz, Michael Downey, Jane Garton, Adèle Hayward, Catherine Rubinstein, David Tombesi-Walton; **Design** Helen Benfield, Darren Hill, Ian Midson, Simon J. M. Oon, Kate Poole, Nicola Webb; **DTP assistance** Rachel Symons; **Consultants** Josephine Bryan, Jane Lyle; **Indexer** Hilary Bird; **Proofreader** David Perry; **Photography** Steve Gorton; **Additional photography** Andy Crawford, Tim Ridley; **Photographers' assistants** Sarah Ashun, Nick Goodall, Lee Walsh; **Illustrators** Joanna Cameron, Yahya El-Droubie, Richard Tibbetts.

Models Felicity Crowe, Patrick Dobbs, Carole Evans, Vosjava Fahkro, John Gillard, Ben Glickman, Zahid Malik, Mutsumi Niwa, Lois Sharland, Daniel Stevens, Fiona Terry, Gilbert Wu; **Make-up** Elizabeth Burrage.

Special thanks to the following for their help throughout the series:
Ron and Chris at Clark Davis & Co. Ltd for stationery and furniture supplies;
Pam Bennett and the staff at Jones Bootmakers, Covent Garden, for the loan of footwear;
Alan Pfaff and the staff at Moss Bros, Covent Garden, for the loan of the men's suits;
and Anna Youle for all her support and assistance.

Suppliers Austin Reed, Church & Co., Compaq, David Clulow Opticians, Elonex, Escada, Filofax, Mucci Bags.

Picture researcher Mariana Sonnenberg; **Picture library assistant** Sam Ward.

PICTURE CREDITS

Key: *b* bottom, *c* centre, *l* left, *r* right, *t* top
Tony Stone Images jacket front cover *tl*, 4–5, 49*br*, 59*bl*, 60*bl*, 61*tr*.

AUTHOR'S BIOGRAPHY

Tim Hindle is founder of the London-based business language consultancy, Working Words, which helps international companies to compose material in English and communicate their messages clearly to their intended audiences. A regular business writer, Tim Hindle has been a contributor to *The Economist* since 1979 and was editor of *EuroBusiness* from 1994 to 1996. As editorial consultant and author, he has produced a number of titles including *Pocket Manager, Pocket MBA,* and *Pocket Finance*, and a biography of Asil Nadir, *The Sultan of Berkeley Square.*